BAG 'EM

and

TAG 'EM

-all about deer huntin'

by Rick Black

3

Preface

If you learn just <u>one thing</u> from this book that helps you bag a monster wall-hanging buck, then the few dollars you shelled out was worth <u>every last cent</u>!

For almost 25 years I have been a Whitetail Deer Hunting fanatic!
I have had the privilege of hunting with some of the best midwestern deer hunters that one could find .

I wrote a venison cook book with great recipes from deer hunters that aged from 18 to 70. If I have learned one thing about whitetail deer hunting, it is that you still learn every time you're on the hunt.

It has been my privilege to hunt with some of the finest deer hunting groups in the Midwest.
It was my wife that convinced me to write this

book. I, by all means, do not claim to be the Daniel Boone of deer hunting, however, I have learned the secrets of the old pros that still produce record keeping whitetail bucks to this day.

It is my purpose to document what the "old boys" say about the tricks of the trade when it comes to bagging that trophy buck.
This book is intended to give advice and tips on how to bag and tag your whitetail deer.

Keeping in mind that though some types of hunting have declined in recent years, I strongly believe that the whitetail deer hunters have a strong and bright future ahead of them.

I have learned throughout the years that your future as a successful deer hunter has much more to do with your knowledge as to how to hunt than it does with luck or the apparent lack of deer in your area.

I do ask, that, as a reader of this book, that you keep one thing in mind. It is up to you to pass on the sport of deer hunting to kids.

Nothing pleases me more than to see our young learning the art of hunting. It is up to us to teach the younger generations the skills and safety involved in outdoor sports such as hunting.

Like our fathers did for us, I believe that in today's fast pace living, hunting provides a special bond between the young and the old.

In this book you will learn the basics of deer hunting. We will cover all the steps needed to bring you within rock shocking range of a wall hanging buck, *heck I even threw in a few of my favorite venison recipes in the back for you to use when you bag your deer!*
Keep in mind that this book is to be used as a tool. Deer hunting is an art that takes time and practice.

Teaching our young such things as respect, law, and appreciation of wildlife can only lead to a better world to live in. This book is written for our young and old sportsman's of America. Enjoy!

Rick Black

Chapter 1

History Of The Whitetail

"There's more to deer hunting than just trying to get a large rack, these deer are faster, smarter and a heck of a lot more knowledgeable of these woods than you are, boy! So pay attention and respect what we are about to hunt.
And for God sakes, tie up your boot string before you fall down and poke your eye out!"
-Richard Black Sr (Dad) 1975

If your going to be a master deer hunter, then your going to need to know a little history lesson about what your hunting!
Scientists believe that deer once inhabited bitter-

cold regions around the Arctic Circle.
It wasn't until about 4 million years ago that the first deer migrated to what we now know as the United States.

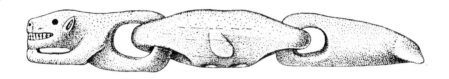

Deer were an integral part of the Native American's lives. Meat and bone marrow made up a large part of their diet.
Indians used the deer hides for clothing, rugs, blankets, fishnets and such.
They crafted arrowheads, clubs, fishhooks and tools out of the bones.

The first settlers of America feasted on various animals, such as turkeys and grouse. Then they discovered the big Virginia whitetail.
Native Americans taught the colonists how to utilize a deer efficiently, using every scrap of meat, hide and bone.

Over time, deer populations have undergone fluctuations. The first big decline was tied to the fur trade.

Native Americans killed an estimated 5 million deer per year to supply the trade. In the early 1880s, due to a decline in fur sales and the natural expansion of deer into new habitats, populations were on the rise again.
However, this increase did not last long.

Rampant market hunting in the late 1800s reduced the whitetail population to an all-time low of 500,000, and does and bucks disappeared completely in parts of the United States.

In 1900 the Lacy Act, the first federal wildlife law, was enacted.

Lacy prohibited the interstate trafficking of venison and other wild game, and the exploitation of the whitetails began to slow.

In 1908, 41 states established departments of conservation, furthering the protection of deer.

The Great Depression was hard on all Americans. But it was a boom time for the whitetails in the East, South and Midwest.

As people flocked from the country to scrap out a living in the towns and cities, abandoned farms

and home sites sprouted weeds, brush and saplings.

Biologists and sportsmen began to realize that America's changing habitat was good for the growing numbers of deer. Once considered denizens of big, contiguous forests, whitetails would now be known as "edge" animals.

In the late 1950s, a biologist named Crockford developed a dart-gun system for capturing deer. That technology, along with future inventions like the cannon net, played a key role in the successful restocking of whitetails across the Untied States.

By 1970 whitetail populations were growing steadily across the lower 48 states.

For years hunters had thought it a crime to shoot a doe.

But a landmark study in 1974 changed that. Scientist M.L. Walls found that the long-term management of booming deer herds should include the harvest of both bucks and does.

States gradually began implementing " doe days" and "antlerless" hunting seasons.

Whitetail populations continued to soar throughout the 1980s and 90s. Solid deer management was one reason.

And then there was suburban sprawl. In many regions more and more people built single-family

homes in once-rural areas, creating a checkerboard of "farmettes" and small estates.

Developers carved subdivisions, golf courses and strip malls of farms and woodlands. Ironically, this created ideal strip and pocket habitats for the very adaptable whitetail, which has an uncanny knack of living alongside man.

This trend continues in the new millennium, and it is not without its downsides.
Burgeoning numbers of deer ravage shrubs, fruit trees and crops, causing hundreds of millions of

dollars in damages annually in the Midwest, Northeast and Southeast.

Deer-auto collisions are on the rise in many states. Today, the whitetail, *Odocoileus virginianus*, is the most widespread deer in the world. Scientists recognize 30 whitetail subspecies in North and Central America, and another eight races in South America.

North America's whitetail population is estimated at 20 – 25 million animals. The whitetail is by far the most popular game in the United States; chased by some 11 million hunters each fall.

Chapter 2

Facts About The Whitetail Deer

" So let me get this straight. You're telling me that this Ted Nugent hippie is a big time deer hunter. If that's the case, then tell me why he wants to scratch cats with fevers? I don't get it! It just don't seem right."
-Richard Black Sr.1978

The average life span for the whitetails in the wild is about ten to fifteen years.
The amazing fact is during much of a whitetail buck's life is spent dodging hunters each fall for his entire adult life. I suppose that is why a mature whitetail buck is very clever when it comes to his environment.
This is why I have chosen to start out with the facts about the whitetail's **_senses_**.

It has been said that a whitetail buck can hear the clicking of a hunters fingernails 100 yards down wind.

With this in mind, I have been told that a whitetail buck can hear a hunter up to a half-mile away.

One must keep this in mind when going to and from a deer stand or blind.

Another thing to focus on is a whitetail's sense of **_eyesight_**.

A whitetail buck has exceptionally good eyesight, especially in semi-darkness.

The pros will tell you that dawn and dusk are the

time periods when you have your best chance of a shot. During these periods of time whitetail's eyesight is far superior to yours.

The advantage of this time period is that a buck will sometimes not notice motionless hunters, however they can spot movement from incredible distances!

This is the time period when the experienced hunter will *stalk walk and use binoculars.*
So let's inform you has to what a "stalk walk" is.
Stalk walking is when a hunter will walk at a very slow pace attempting to minimize sound and movement.

When stalk walking a seasoned hunter will walk *heel to toe.*

Moving at very slow pace, the hunter will avoid

the sounds of leaves and sticks that may snap crackle and alert, the whitetail of your location. Your binoculars will come in to place while you are engaged on your stalk walk.
This will give you a chance to *"scope"* your surroundings.

An experienced hunter will stop about every 10 yards and do a 180 searching for a whitetail rack above the grass and timber.

I have shot about 70 percent of my large bucks by following this routine.

To sum it up, keep in mind that the whitetail buck can spot movement from incredible distances. Keep in mind that a whitetail buck is much superior to man in physical endowments and instinct.

With this knowledge the smart deer hunter will recognize that the only advantage they have over a deer is the factor of reasoning.

And remember, that the difference between an average deer hunter and a pro is the ability to outsmart the deer.

This brings us to ***speed.*** The whitetail deer is a quick runner.

Some say that a buck in a full run can move or run from danger at speeds up to 40 miles an hour. Along with this is the fact that a whitetail can jump up to 15 feet in the air!

And if that's not enough, you can take into consideration the fact that a whitetail can swim up to the speeds to about 30 miles an hour!

We have read about the incredible talents of the whitetail. We learned that a whitetail buck can hear a hunter up to 100 yards, and that a whitetail has excellent eyesight.

The whitetail can jump up to 15 feet in the air, along with the fact that a white tail can swim a river or lake up to 30 miles an hour!
Because of this, I truly believe that the whitetail buck is a master of **_Survival Instinct._**

The breeding conditions **_"Rut"; _** in the Midwest and the Northern states are from September to February.

However, the midwestern buck hunter will tell you *"Rut"* is from October to December.

An aggressive buck will travel many miles in search of a doe in heat.

One amazing fact is that a female white tail *"Doe"* can become pregnant at the age of six months and may continue to bear *fawns* after she is ten years old.

A bit of good news for the whitetail hunter is the fact that male deer outnumber the female deer about 110 to 100 at birth.

Buck fawns are also stronger and weigh more than their sisters.

Yearling does produce an average of two deer a year.

The gestation period is about 200 days.

Now we begin with ***Habitat.*** One thing to keep in mind is that the whitetail buck living in ideal terrain may cover only a mile or two from his place of birth.

This is why the old boys search for "sheds", A shed is a white tail buck's rack that has fallen off during the winter months.

I once went shed hunting with a Deer hunting buddy, when he found a ***200-point Bone and Crocket Iowa record.***

Needless to say, I tried to arm wrestle him for it, but because he found both right and left sheds, he would not even think about the fact of losing his find.

Next is ***Body Language.*** A whitetail's intentions are often revealed by its body language.
It is important to know these specific reactions and use them to be a more successful hunter.
Keep note that when a deer wags its tail stiffly in a horizontal plane it is often used as an "all clear sign" signal, alerting other deer that danger has passed and they can come out of hiding.

One must keep in mind that similar swishing of the tail can also indicate relaxation.
In this case the deer tail is not stiff or is it held in an upright position.

When a whitetail deer wags its tail in this way, it means it is not alerted to danger.
It is important to keep track on the deer's scratching and interaction with other deer.

A feeding deer will always twitch its tail before raising its head to look around for danger. This is good to keep in mind if you are stalking the deer.

A whitetail buck that stamps its hoofs on the ground is most likely telling nearby deer one of two things.

1. The deer is upset about nearby danger.
2. The buck can sense competition with a rival buck.

The deer that is unalarmed will normally carry its tail low; however the first sign of danger it will raise it like a white flag.

In closing to this chapter. It is important that deer hunter knows that deer cover much of the country and are one of the most hunted large games.

Chances are good that if a hunter hunts anything other than birds, they hunt deer.

The whitetail is named for its most distinctive feature, the large white tail or flag that is often all a hunter will see as it bounds away. Its belly and the underside of its tail are completely white, and it has a white patch on the throat.

Yearling bucks average about 150 pounds. Older bucks will weigh in at 200 pounds or more when field dressed.

Antler development is dependant on nutrition. The typical whitetail buck antler has a main beam that sweeps forward and each of the points rise from it. Antler growth begins normally in April to early May.

Knowing your game and how it behaves will greatly increase your success rates when hunting. Stealth, the right gun or bow, a steady aim, knowledge, and perseverance all play a role in your success.

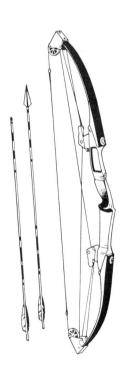

Chapter 3

Preparation For The Hunt

*" See, what did I tell you about fresh snow on ladder
stands! You just had a dumb attack #3. Now get up, wipe
yourself off, and don't put your tongue on the barrel
again this year! And get a haircut! And for the last time,
you don't have an Uncle named Ted!"*
-Richard Black Sr. 1981

Mental Preparation - Hunting, like all sports,
requires mental preparation. Many novices get
discouraged when they don't get their bucks.
But these hunters fail to understand that thousands
of skilled deer hunters scout, monitor deer herds
and practice shooting year-round. And come fall,

many of them also don't bag big bucks.

So prepare your gear, scout, practice your shooting and hit the timber with the right frame of mind.

Don't expect to shoot a Boone and Crocket – class buck every season.

Some years you'll have to be content to fill your freezer with a small buck or doe.

But that is **alright**. It is the thrill of the hunt and chase.

If scouting were only done a few weeks before deer hunting started, it would be basically a shot in the dark when deciding to put up the tree stand.

But if the deer's locations were known throughout the year, and you knew they always stayed in a certain area of the timber when hunting season commenced, that would then be the most logical place to put up your stand.

That gives you higher chances for bagging a large buck.

License Permits - In any state or province you need a big game license to hunt deer.
Some states require a special archery or muzzle-loading license. In Iowa, Illinois, Kansas, Montana and other states you must apply for a buck only tag, generally in the spring or early summer.
You must check the state and it's regulations carefully before the hunting season.
Keep in mind that some states let you purchase a license online or by telephone.

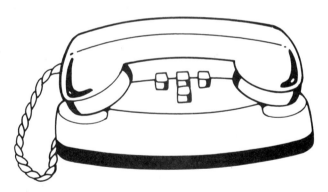

Clothing - Hunting clothes should be comfortable and quiet.
They should keep you warm and dry in inclement weather. Gore-Tex, wool and fleece are recommended.

In warn weather, cotton clothes are what the pros recommend.

Remember to spray down your clothes with a scent killer so deer won't smell you. Or wear a Scent-Lock suit. (Tip) Always keep your camo clothing in plastic bags to keep them as odorless as possible.

Camouflage – Even though deer have excellent sight, they are mostly colorblind.

Deer see in shades of black and white, and that is why camouflage is very effective.

A pattern blends with the black – gray background of the timber and helps to break your outline.

Still, camouflaged hunters must minimize movements or risk of being seen by the whitetail.

There are many different camouflages and patterns. The most common is the "bark" pattern, like Realtree, Mossy Oak and Natural Gear.

Most states require fluorescent orange during gun season.

Deer cannot detect the orange but other hunters see it easily for safety.

Many hunters camouflage their bodies, but forget about their face and hands. This is a huge mistake!

Keep in mind that your head and hands move a lot, and that movement can spook an incoming buck.

Wear camo gloves and a face mask (or paint) especially when bow hunting or calling up the big buck.

Footwear – The number one thing above all else, boots should keep your feet warm and dry, and provide good traction.

Many hunters prefer all-rubber or rubber-bottomed boots, which help minimize the scent you leave on the ground.

If you wear leather boots, spray them with an order-neutralizer.

One tip on buying boots: Purchase a pair a half-size larger than you normally wear.

That way you can wear extra socks and stick in chemical foot warmers.

Keep in mind that if your boots are too tight, your feet will get cold very quickly. *Socks are just as*

important. Wear thin liners that wick away sweat, and top the liners with wool socks.

Safety Knowledge – Know your deer – hunting firearm inside and out.

Know how to properly load it, carry it, fire it and clean it.

Be careful with a firearm; there should be no such words as a "hunting accident" in you vocabulary!

I highly recommend you know basic survival, first aid and CPR.

Carry the proper equipment; First aid kit, compass, matches, knife and map of where you are hunting.

Always carry spare gloves and socks. Always tell someone where you are planning to hunt and when you plan to get back to camp or home. This could be a vital backup in case you get lost or injured.

Before hunting for the first time, take a hunter Education Course. This is required in most states for all young sportsmen.

Equipment – When deer hunting close to home, you can get by with a daypack or a fanny pack. In a more remote area you might need a frame backpack.

You can carry many items in a pack, but never leave camp or home without the follow hunting essentials:

- Waterproof matches or lighter
- Flashlight

- Knife with sharpening stone
- Safety belt (for tree stand hunting)
- Maps and compass
- Flagging tape
- First aid kit
- Spare eyeglasses or contacts
- Raingear
- Spare socks, gloves and jacket
- Portable Deer stand
- Extra ammo

- Scent cover
- Paper towels
- Tissue paper
- Cell phone (keep it off while hunting)
- Tools for weapon adjustments
- Watch
- Binoculars
- Latex gloves (for gutting)

Believe it or not. I can get all of these items in and on my backpack. There has not been an item listed that I have not had to use in my 25 years of hunting.

Chapter 4

Deer Hunting Weapons

"Happiness is a warm gut pile on a cold winters' day!
Now drag this big boy out for the old man."
-Richard Black Sr. 1982

General Information

There is a wide assortment of deer hunting weapons, including high-powered rifles, shotguns, muzzleloaders, handguns and bows.
Sometimes a hunter has the privilege of choosing which weapon to use.
For instance, hunters may choose to further challenge themselves by using a bow and arrow or

a muzzleloader during the general gun season. However, during specific seasons, such as archery deer or muzzleloader, regulations prohibit the use of high-powered or shotgun firearms.

The gun of choice for most whitetail hunters is the centerfire rifle, perhaps a bolt-action chambered for .270 or .30-06.
It's ease of operation and extreme accuracy makes it the most dependable of all deer hunting firearms.

However, some states prohibit the use of high-powered rifles in heavily populated urban areas.

In these situations, the shotgun or muzzleloader is used for safety reasons.

These two firearms have good killing power and accuracy up to around 100 yards.
After that, a heavy slug or conical bullet loses velocity and drops off dramatically; thereby expending it's energy before it travels within range of nearby dwellings.

A select few sportsmen opt for the high-powered pistol. Now holding a handgun on a buck and trying to deliver a killing shot is a true hunter's task.
There are many states talking about a specific handgun season. But for now, if your heart is set on getting a deer with a handgun you'll have to join the ranks with rifle hunters during a modern firearms season.

The bow & arrow is an efficient hunting tool out to around 35 yards or so.
As such, special archery only seasons are the norm in September or October.

A growing number of archers opt to use their bows and arrows during general firearms seasons. But then they must compete with the crowds of gun hunters.
Some states hold late season archery – only hunt. Giving bow hunters one last crack at tagging bucks.

Now while on the subject of weapons, lets talk about your hunting knife.
Have you ever noticed the more experienced the hunter, the smaller the knife they carry. Why?

Because you don't need a blade longer than four inches or so to perfectly execute the gutting, skinning, quartering, and caping of your deer.

A good knife is small, sharp, and handy. Those Bowies with the 12 –inch blades may look good swinging from your belt, but when it comes to field dressing a deer they are nothing but awkward.

Furthermore, all you need is a sharp blade. You don't need long finger guards, blood grooves, saw backs, finger grips in the handles, double edges, double hilts, or any of the other gimmicks that range from silly to downright dangerous.

So get a top-quality knife with a blade of four inches or so and you'll be perfectly equipped. Anything else is excess weight.

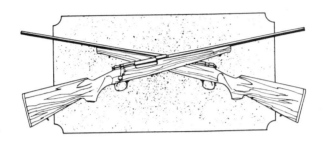

The Rifle – The centerfire rifle is the favorite weapon of deer hunters. Riffle hunters take some 80% of all the whitetails killed each fall.
And that percentage would be even higher except that many urban areas allow only shotguns or muzzleloaders for safety reasons.

For many hunter, the modern rifle has become more than a tool to harvest a deer. Many of today's rifles, especially the custom type, are works of art, complete with beautiful stock work and metalwork.

Many hunters choose to reload their own centerfire shells, not so much to save money, but to further enjoy the hunting experience. There is a special satisfaction in knowing that you loaded the shell that delivered pinpoint accuracy and brought down your buck.

When properly sighted in with a good load, a modern scoped rifle can yield 3-shot groups of an inch or less at 100 yards. Accuracy is the main reason most hunters prefer to hunt deer with a high-powered rig.

Rifle Calibers – Many rifle calibers will kill a large buck, from the diminutive .22 long rifle to the shoulder-thumping .338 magnum. However, sportsmen over the years have chosen a handful of cartridges as favorites for whitetails.

The 270 Winchester is one of the most popular
deer hunting weapons.
This flat-shooting round zips a 150-grain bullet
along at about 2800 feet per second. Many hunters
prefer the lighter 130 – grain load because of
recoil is slightly less and the bullet trajectory is
flatter.

The .30-30 is a short-range deer gun. Because of
the rainbow trajectory of its bullets, a 200-yard
shot and the knock down power of this large
caliber weapon allows deer hunters a good harvest

in thick hardwood timber. For ranges of 100 yards
or less, the old .30-30 remains a favorite.
The .30-06 is my personal choice. More deer
hunters carry the .30-06 than any other caliber,
and for good reason.

Loads vary from the 110-grainer for varmints to
the 220-grainer for grizzly bear.
The .30-06 is so universally accepted that it is the
most sought out rifle in about every sporting
goods store in the United States.

The Shotgun – Shotgun deer seasons occur throughout populated areas of the Eastern, South and Midwest.

Years ago, hunters used the same shotgun to hunt both birds and bucks. There were no fancy, specialized slug guns with fiber-optic sights or scopes, just smoothbores with pointing beads.

The results were predictable. Many of hunters missed a lot of bucks standing broadside at 20 yards!

All that has changed. Guns with rifled barrels, shooting rifled slugs, are highly accurate and have greatly improved the hunters' odds during shotgun season.

Many of today's shot gunners are taking a tip from the muzzle loading hunters and using sabot bullets.

Another great addition to the slug gun is the scope. An optic makes shooting a deer at 100 yards, once thought to be impossible for a shotgun, both possible and probable.

Shotgun Calibers – Most shotguns manufactured specifically for deer hunters are chambered for 12 gauge, though some guns are available in 20 gauge.

The 12-gauge slug is big and powerful, though a bit slow. Ammo manufacturers have helped to solve this problem by introducing sabot bullets. A sabot is a plastic shroud that holds a smaller bullet.

For instance, you might use in a 12-gauge shotgun, which has a ¾ -inch bore diameter, a saboted .44 magnum jacketed bullet.

The lighter bullet will fly faster and flatter than an all-lead slug at 100 yards.

In congested areas, some states allow only buckshot for deer.

Buckshot loads consist of several lead balls inside a 3-inch shotgun shell.

Buckshot loads can be very deadly out to 40 yards or so, but after that, their energy is largely spent. Keep in mind that only buckshot loads can be used in smoothbore shotguns.

The Muzzleloader – The muzzleloading rifle has gained great popularity in the past decade.

All but two states now have special deer seasons set aside for black-powder hunters.

One allure of muzzleloading is the feeling of getting back to the old days when hunters were responsible for bringing home game.

Generally, muzzleloading rifles fall into two groups; traditional and modern.

The traditional rifle is a replica of the long rifle that the settlers used 200 years ago. The rifle has a front and rear sight for aiming. A side hammer sparks a flint stone, sending sparks onto the black powder in a frizzen pan.

The charge is then transferred to the main charge of black powder.

A more popular version of the replica rifle is the percussion; the side hammer strikes a percussion cap rather than a flint.

A hunter can expect fair to good accuracy with these traditional rifles out to about 80 yards or so. The guns occasionally have firing problems when moisture gets onto the frizzen pan or into a percussion nipple.

The modern muzzleloader must be hand-loaded down the barrel just like a traditional rifle. All similarities end there.

The "in-line" muzzleloader looks and shoots much like a centerfire rifle.

It contains an enclosed breech and firing pin.

Calibers - Muzzleloading deer rifles come in 3 calibers: .45, .50 and the 54. Most whitetail hunters prefer the .50, while elk and moose hunters sometimes scale up to the bigger .54.

Much of the performance of any black-powder rifle depends on the loading charge.
A light change of black powder or pyrodex will not produce a very fast-moving bullet, especially when you consider the fact that most bullets weigh about ¾ ounce.

Many black-powder hunters now use the saboted bullet. This bullet I had explained earlier in the "shotgun" section of this chapter, however I will inform you again.

The sabot bullet for the .50 caliber might hold a .45 caliber handgun bullet.

The decrease in bullet weight leads to a marked increase in velocity, which extends range and improves accuracy because of less bullet drop.

Generally, any caliber of modern muzzleloader can produce decent accuracy up to 100 yards or so.

Along with the primer to fire the main charge, modern black powder guns are drilled and tapped for scopes. In addition, the modern muzzleloader can use the accurate and hard-hitting sabot bullet.

I, like most hunters, appreciate the old black powder way of hunting. However, I highly recommend the "in-line" muzzleloader for advantage over today's trophy bucks.

Bow & Arrow – Archery hunting is called the ultimate challenge because the sportsman purposely limits himself with the short-range bow and arrow.

Instead of a gun ending a hunt when a distant deer is seen, the bow hunter's challenge has just begun.

An archer must use his woodsmanship and wiles to either stalk within 30 yards of a deer or wait until it tips into bow range.

The adrenalin rush is incredible as a big buck slowly, finally, saunters within good killing range. Even when a big buck is close, harvest is not a sure thing.

The exaggerated movements to pick up and draw a bow, plus many intangibles like a swirling wind,

work against the archer.
Then there are the whitetail's acute senses, which are magnified at extremely close range.

More often than not deer escape unharmed, but most archery hunters shrug it off with a smile or grin.
Certainly the challenge of the hunt and the excitement of a point-blank encounter with a buck are the driving forces that make people pick up their bows and head for the timber for deer.

Word has gotten around about the excitement. Of the roughly 17 million hunters in America, some 11 million people hunt deer and more than 3.5 million of those use a bow.

In fact, bow and arrow hunting for whitetails is one of the fastest growing outdoor sports.

Most states offer archery-only seasons that open in September or October, before gun hunters spook and shoot the deer. You can literally double your fun in the timber by archery hunting in early fall, and then gun hunt later in the season.

Types of Bows – There are 3 types of hunting bows. Longbow, recurve and compound.
All have their good points; archers kill lots of deer with each type every year.
However, there are distinct differences between the bows that you should consider before purchasing or hunting with one.

The longbow is a throwback to the old days of archery hunting.
During the infancy years of bow hunting back in the 1920s, the only bows used were the longbows in the six-foot range.

The longbow is, above all else, simplicity in motion.
An archer simply strings the bow, draws back the arrow and shoots. Virtually all of longbow shooting is instinctive, meaning no distance sights are used.

On the downside, the longbow is notoriously slow. An arrow shot from a 60- pound pull longbow will poke along at about 150 feet per second.

That is slow enough for a deer to spook and be gone before an arrow gets there!
Generally the purist who is into the nostalgia of archery shoots the longbow.

The recurve is so named because the tips of the bow curve backwards, giving the bow extra casting power.

The recurve was the answer to the complaint that the longbow was too slow.

Today's modern recurves are crafted of laminated wood and fiberglass, which combine to produce an efficient bow.
A 60-pound recurve with a fast-flight string will shoot an arrow at about 200 feet per second. That's almost 50 feet per second faster than a longbow with the same draw weight.

Consequently, the recurve is a good choice for the traditional archer who wants a little more arrow speed than the longbow can produce.

About 85% of all bow hunters use the compound bow because it is efficient and very accurate. Screw on a good bow sight and excellent accuracy at 30 to 40 yards is very possible. But still, to this day, hunters who have learned to shoot instinctively prefer the recurve because it does not need to be constantly tuned and calibrated like the high-tech compound bow.

The Handgun – At this time, I am not aware of any specific handgun-only seasons in the states for the whitetail deer.

However, many hunters harvest deer with large caliber pistols during general rifle or shotgun seasons.

Of course, these sportsmen are aware that they enjoy the challenge of shooting a pistol and having to get close to bucks. I have hunted deer with all types of the above named weapons. With that I can truly say, I enjoy handgun hunting the best.

Calibers – Most calibers used for deer hunting are large bore with a large kick.

The .357 magnum is one of the best because it doesn't recoil too much, yet it packs enough power to drop a big buck on his keester!

A 150-grain .357 load has a muzzle velocity of about 1600 feet per second.

Most serious pistol hunters choose the .44 mag. It packs a big kick and a big bang, two factors that tend to adversely affect accuracy unless a shooter practices a lot.

A 220 grain .44 magnum load has the muzzle velocity of about 1900 feet per second. Some hunters go for the .41 magnum, which has almost as much power as the .44 but not the tremendous kick.

The Thompson Contender is a designed – for-hunting handgun that breaks the mold of the typical revolving cylinder pistol. Any hunter who wants to harvest a buck with a pistol should check it out.

The Contender actually utilizes a tiny bolt action, and has a breech much like a single-shot rifle. The Contender accepts most high-powered rifle cartridges, such as the .270, .30-30 and .30-06. *Boy's, this is one bad Momma!* The Contender also allows for interchangeable barrels, another reason it is one of the best choices for deer hunting!

Chapter 5

The Art of Still - hunting

"I told you to go before we left the camp!
You're just going to have to hold it!
ROOKIES!"
-Richard Black Sr. 1982

Still-hunting is probably the least understood of all deer-hunting techniques.

To begin with, the term is a misnomer. It would seem to imply that a person hunts by remaining still. In some states in the Southeast this definition is still in vogue.

If a hunter in that area tells you they got their

buck while still-hunting they probably mean that they shot the animal while sitting still on a stand.

The basic concept of still-hunting is moving slowly and as quietly as possible while looking for deer you suspect to be in the area.

In contrast, stalking means moving slowly and quietly as possible while trying to sneak within shooting range of a buck you have already spotted.
Still-hunting can change into stalking on a second's notice when you suddenly spot your buck unless the stalker blows the chance and has to resort to finding another buck.

Still-hunting won't work in heavily hunted timber.

You need solitude. In an area where there are many hunters there just isn't the room to practice sneaking tactics because there's too much human interference with normal movement patterns of deer.
In dense timber it's too difficult to move quietly and almost impossible to see far ahead.

If you hunt under such conditions it's always better to use a stand.
The more open country of the West and Southwest is still where still-hunting works best.

The intriguing thing about still-hunting is that the action is explosive. Of all the deer I've killed, some of the bucks I remember best hit the ground while I was still-hunting.

The still-hunter must sneak in among the deer, and this calls for all the skill, stealth, and caution a hunter can muster. The very nature of the game implies that you'll occasionally come upon deer that are unaware of you until you get very close.

More often you'll come upon deer that are very much aware of your presence, but these animals choose to try hiding till they no longer can stand the tension of a nearby human.

In any event, the shocking thrill of deer exploding from cover at close range is almost always an

adventure reserved for the still-hunter.
It sometimes happens to stalkers, less often to drivers, and still less frequently to standers.

A stalker may ease onto a deer while sneaking up on another.
A driver seldom experiences the explosive dashing of a deer because they cannot travel silently enough to get close without alerting them.
A stander is stationary except for the travel needed to get to their stand, so the opportunity for jumping deer is greatly diminished.

To still- hunt properly in thick cover, you take a half-dozen slow steps and then stop to look and listen.

During the stops you should look to your right and scan on a distant plane in an arc to your left.

Then drop your line of view a few yards and scan on the same plane from left to right.

Drop the sight plane again and continue inspecting the terrain ahead back and forth. The idea is to check out ever piece of cover from the horizon to a few yards in front of you.

What you are trying to do is see deer before they see you, or to see them before they become nervous enough to jump and move out. Learning to spot deer when doing this takes time and skill.

If you travel more than a mile an hour you're not still-hunting properly; you're just taking a walk.

The old boys say that you can't still-hunt at more than a half a mile per hour and expect to see the details your eyes must interpret to spot motionless deer.

They claim that if you move at a faster pace you're bound to make too much noise to sneak in on a target. Which brings up another aspect of the misnomer of still-hunting.

Since a still-hunter is moving, however so slowly, they are bound to make some sounds.
You should take it for granted that deer usually hear you because their keen ears pick up every approaching sound.

There is no such thing as a completely noiseless approach.

And herein lies one of the most important secrets of still-hunting.

The key is that game itself isn't noiseless. A deer moving down a runway makes sound, but they're natural sounds if another deer hears them because they expect to hear them on game trails.

The same deer would not expect to hear off-trail sounds, especially if they were loud and persistent.

So the sounds of movement can be natural or unnatural, and deer positively know the difference. Another advantage of stopping so often is that you get a chance to use your ears.

If you're dead still you have the opportunity of hearing deer that would otherwise sneak away without disclosing their presence.

One thing to keep in mind is that there is no sense in still-hunting an area that doesn't harbor deer.
A good bet is to scout for recently used bedding areas.
When you hunt a bedding area you should try to determine which trail the deer use in reaching it.

For example, no unalarmed deer will travel downwind.
If you approach a bedding area along a downwind trail, a buck will immediately become alerted to

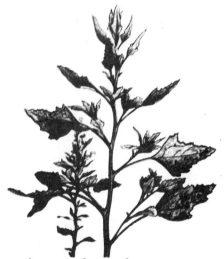

the unnatural sounds and movements that wouldn't concern him if you were traveling a trail in an upwind direction.

The basic rule is always to still-hunt with the wind in your face or partially in your face.

Still – Hunting in Pairs- Many deer hunters have the mistaken idea that only lone hunters must practice still-hunting.

This thought is based on the principle that one hunter will make only half the noise of two.

Well, this principle isn't necessarily true. Two hunters can actually make less noise than one.

The trick is to use hand signals to eliminate all talking or whispering.

The main thing is for one hunter to move ahead about 100 feet, concentrating entirely on traveling silently.
His attention is riveted on not stepping on sticks or dry leaves or brushing against branches.

The stationary hunter watches for deer while the other travels.
Then the lead hunter watches while his partner moves up.

The system is very time-consuming, but it combines the twin advantages of practically noiseless travel with having one set of eyes and ears that are always alert for deer.
With this technique two hunters can hunt more efficiently than one.

Chapter 6

Driving As a Group
"My God Billy! Roll down the window, and lay off the deer chili!"
-Rick Black, every season

Years ago the old-fashioned gang drive was one of the best techniques for producing venison anywhere in whitetail country.
It worked well in those days because when deer were jumped they ran for their lives.

They ran straight away from the drivers and into the sights of the standers who were posted ahead of the drivers. In those times of less hunting pressure than we have today, deer were startled at the mere presence of a hunter.

The naïve little critters bolted as soon as they realized hunters were in their area.

It's all a new ball game today. Modern bucks that flee for safety without thinking about the consequences wind up in freezers.
Those that make it through their first hunting season have learned that the way to stay alive is not to run but to hide or sneak.

That's precisely why the old-time gang drive with a line of hunters moving aimlessly through good deer timber, is seldom productive today.

The keys to success of the modern drive are organization and leaving nothing to chance.

There is another factor most drivers overlook. Many hunters figure there are fewer bucks today than years ago because they don't see as many. In the old days 90 percent of the bucks ran as soon as they realized a hunter was headed toward them.

Today 90 percent will lie still and hope the hunter will walk by.
So how do you cure this problem? The answer is several drivers working closely together while covering the driven area slowly and thoroughly.

They've got to work out every thicket. The more hunters a buck has to cope with, the closer they are together, the slower they move, and the more thoroughly they work the cover, the more nervous the deer will get.

The more nervous a buck gets, the more likely he is to move out. Then you got yourself a wall hanger!
Did you ever wonder why the whitetail harvest in most states is highest the first two days of each new season?

I'm convinced that when the hordes of deer hunters first move into the timbers and the shots start roaring, many of the deer panic.

They're caught by surprise.
The ones that make mistakes get shot. The ones that survive figure out what's going on and they adapt by hiding or moving into remote areas.

The principle is that if you can hunt a buck when he doesn't know what's going on, you have him at a disadvantage, and that's when the drivers can move him.

This happens early in the season, but it also happens when the timbers are damp or covered with a few inches of fresh snow.

If a buck can hear hunters moving, he has little fear.

His extremely sharp sense of hearing enables him to place himself where he'll be out of trouble. This is why so many modern deer sneak back through drives without ever being seen.

However, if you get the conditions where hunters can walk up quietly, especially if it's windy, deer often go wild because they realize danger can be upon them at any moment. It's the unknown that makes them commit errors and move out ahead of a drive.

I have found that our harvest of large bucks always goes up dramatically when new snow is on the ground.
This is the best time to make a drive. Not only because the sounds of the drivers are reduced, but also because deer can be seen more easily against a snow background.

To sum it up in short, if a buck can't be sure where the drivers are and he can't be sure whether or not he'll be seen, he's much more likely to get on the move.

Every good driver I've have talked with claims that good planning is the key to a successful drive. Lets use an example;

Let's say that we have 50 acres of oak trees loaded with acorns and dotted with thickets of brush large enough for bedding areas.
The oaks are surrounded on all sides by dense cedar swamps.

Though the oaks and thickets may harbor the deer, there is not a chance in the world of driving them efficiently because they can sneak out to safety in any direction.

<u>Note-</u> When driven up heavy timber bordered by open ridges, clever bucks will usually hold to the ravine cover and head for an established escape route near the top.

Many things are involved here. Standers must be on their sites before the drive begins or all effort may be wasted.

The obvious example is when deer are moved past sites before the watchers reach them.
Without complete knowledge of the terrain to be driven, the drivers can't know where the standers

will be or how long it will take them to get there.

**The Sweep** – The sweep drive is modified to fit modern conditions.

A sweep drive sweeps around a pivot man – (stander), who locates in cover on a point of land or on a hill where he has a good view.

The drivers closest to the pivot man have to move very slowly because they don't cover much distance as the drive seeps around, but the men on the far side of the line must move at a faster rate

established game trails to get where they want to go.

Knowing this, many of the old boys that got a lot of drives under their boots, check the beginning sections of their driven area after the drive is over.

When they find fresh tracks of deer that had sneaked through the drive they note the routes the deer used to escape.
Then, the next time the area is driven, the "dropout" technique is used.

As the drive progresses a couple of men will drop out along the escape trails and take up stands as the other drivers continue forward.

Many of today's bigger bucks, who assumed they had long ago figured out how to outwit any drive, wind up as a shoulder mount hanging on the hunter's wall.

Any type of drive is guerrilla warfare on deer. You're in close to the deer and your fellow hunters. When the drivers kick up deer, shooting and slugs are a flying.

Wear <u>BLAZE-ORANGE!</u> Don't shoot your buddy, even if he has a good-looking old lady

that can make a mean pan of biscuits. In any case, you get my point. Safety First!

Chapter 7

Tree Stand Hunting

" Man,Rick, today sucked. My feet hurt, I'm cold, I missed the big one, and I got doe urine on my sandwich. So tell me one of them stupid deer hunting jokes your always writing about in your books and cheer me up. "
- ***Darren Crandle 1990***

Tree stand hunters kill thousands of whitetails each fall.

The reason is very clear: A hunter stalking on the ground is easily heard, seen or smelled by the deer.

But a hunter up in a tree stand is quiet and essentially unseen.

The tree stand technique can position a big buck right into your sights.

Stand hunting works in any weather, be it calm, rainy, snowy or during dry times when the ground and your boots make more noise than a Ted Nugent concert.

Tree stand hunting is one of the only methods that can be applied in all conditions. The stand hunter must learn three major skills. The first and most important is where to position a perch. If your stand is not in high-use deer area you can't see them.

Secondly, how you enter and exit a stand area without disturbing the environment is critical.

If a buck hears, smells, or sees you before you get into your stand you will most likely not see that buck again.

Thirdly, you must learn how long to hunt a particular area until it's time to relocate.

It takes a lot of patience to tree stand hunt. Keep in mind that tree stand hunting is an effective way to harvest a large buck.

A lot of planning goes into the tree stand process. Finding the right stand location is a complicated procedure.

It starts out with discovering an area bucks like.

Then you must learn the buck's daily pattern as to set your stand in a spot where the buck is likely to show.

Always keep in mind that stand hunting is the most effective method of deer hunting. Stand hunting is a simple way to hunt. The hunter stays in one spot and watches for deer movement. And because the hunter is not moving, he can sight a deer before the deer even knows what hit him.

A stand hunter should never get too relaxed or quit hunting.
The stand hunter should always be looking for deer movement in the timber that holds the bucks.

A well-seasoned tree stand hunter will spend the entire day watching the area. The hunter knows that a buck will sooner or latter walk within range of his stand.

There really is no one proper height for a tree stand. How high varies depending on the hunter and the terrain.
Most hunters like to be high, 15 feet or more in their tree.

I would recommend not going under 10 feet. At this height the deer will easily spot you and will avoid your area. I also feel that any lower will defeat the propose of the tree stand itself. Remember your there to be unseen.

Another good point is to consider cover when you're setting up your stand.
Try to hang the stand where limbs and leaves will help break up your outline. Low limbs and ground foliage will be a factor, especially when setting up for bow hunting.

Set your stand at a height where you can clearly see incoming deer and get the best shot. If need be, clear out 4 or 5 good shooting lanes. Don't set up and not be able to get a clear shoot at your buck because of obstacles in your shooting path.

I have seen many of well covered, cool looking stands in trees and wondered how the hunter could even see his feet let alone get off a 30 yard shot. Take your time and do it right, it will pay off in the end.

Generally, a stand should be placed in one of two locations.
The best place to stand hunt is overlooking one or more deer runs to move from feeding to bedding.

A rifle hunter can get on a high point and watch over several deer runs in different draws because of the long-range capability of his gun.
However a bow hunter should look for main deer runs that cross and place his stand close to this intersection.

Another good location to place your stand is at a deer's feeding area, such as corn or soybean field.

I once saw a hunter in the middle of a cornfield on a tri-pod stand shoot a monster 14 pointer.
This hunter was smart. He knew his area of hunting. He knew that there would be another hunting party starting a drive next to the field he was in, and he knew that chances of a large buck would choose to take the open field for escape.

This hunter could have had the same results with a tree stand at the edge of the cornfield and timber, however he went with the tri-pod and now has bragging rights for a wall hanger.

Another major factor for considering where to place your stand is wind direction.
Keep in mind that if the wind is blowing from the stand toward the direction of the deer, you'll be lucky to even see a squirrel.

The old boys that tree stand usually have several alternative stand locations.
If the wind is wrong at one stand, they can move to another stand where the wind is not a factor.

The tree stand hunter spends most of the day without moving around.
In cold weather, he must dress adequately to avoid getting the chill and shakes.

Wear insulated boots that will keep your feet warm.
Loose pants and coats, which help trap your body heat, are better than tight fitting clothes.
Don't be afraid to overdress a bit. You can always shed a layer as the day warms on. However, don't wear too many clothes on the walk to your stand or you'll get hot and sweaty, which will cause you to freeze latter on your stand.

Wear good gloves or mittens to keep your hands warm.
Don't use bulky ones that will interfere with your ability to draw back on a bow or fire off a shot.

The old boys use lightweight gloves on their shooting hand and carry hand warmers in their coat pockets.

I myself use a mitten with a lip that flips up and exposes all my fingers when the deer approaches. I found these at a sporting goods store about 5 years ago. At the time they were pretty costly, however now you can pick up a good pair for about $10.00.

Most bow – killed deer are harvested from a tree stand, which provides three major advantages. First an elevated stand offers a good view of the surrounding terrain and brush.

Second, your scent often floats above a buck's sensitive nose. And last, you're above a deer's sight line, though bucks will still look up. Stand installation used to be a long, arduous job, but with today's easy to use tree stands and steps, a bow hunter can accomplish the chore in about 20 minutes.

There are many excellent portable stands on the market.
Some are small, simple devices that can be hung up quickly, while other types are larger and require more work.
But these bad boys are very roomy and comfortable.

With a fixed-position stand you have the option of using screw – in stapes or ladder steps, which have multiple rungs and hook to a tree with straps. There are climbing stands; you work your way quickly up a tree using the "stand up, sit down" method.

Climbers work the best in areas with straight trees that have few low growing branches.
As I stated earlier, I would, at least hang your stand about 15 or more feet from the ground. That's high enough to get your scent, outline and movements above the deer's eyes, ears, and nose.

Unlike the bow hunter who relies almost totally on the tree stand to kill his buck, the gun hunter benefits from the greater range and accuracy of his hunting weapon, so he is not as concerned with deer seeing or smelling him at close range.

Still, a tree stand provides definite advantages for the gun hunter, and more gun hunters are discovering the benefits of the tree stand hunting techniques.

The greatest benefit is the increased visibility. In many areas where ground brush cuts vision to 25 yards or less, the gun hunter who climbs into a tree stand positioned above the canopy of brush can often see for a hundred yards or more.

In addition, a tree stand allows a gun hunter to sit in comfort while he spends the day scanning the timber for deer activity.

And when a deer is spotted, a steady gun rest can usually be taken from a tree stand.

Most gun tree stands are located looking over a large area where a hunter can see the deer from a distance and use the ballistics and accuracy of his firearm to drop a buck at longer ranges.

However, like I stated earlier, take note of the wind direction.

It is a well-known fact that a whitetail buck can smell human scent well over 150 yards away. For all tree stand hunters, having the correct accessories for the job is a must!
For tree stand hunting, I highly recommend the following accessories:

Safety belt – To be used for hanging and climbing into tree stands. Strap into a stand with a belt or chest harness.

Binoculars – A great tool for glassing the area for deer.

Fanny Pack – *Kleenex* for runny noses. Deer can hear sniffing. *Food and drink* should be brought because you're going to be spending a lot of time up in your stand.

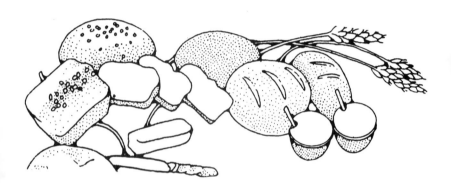

Sunglasses – The sun and snow can make hunters eyes very tried and sore.

Hook – Use a hook to hang the bow or gun on when not using it.

Tree pegs / steps – Used to climb the stand.

Orange safety ribbon – Used to lay out at different yardage for judging if deer are within shooting range.

Carpet – Use carpet to lay on the bottom of your stand to minimize noises from your boots.

Wire saw – Used to remove small branches or limbs that block your view or shooting path.

Rope – Used to pull up your weapon and equipment.

Chapter 8

Trails, Buck Fever, and Odor Control

" Mr. Black, for the last time. Quit referring to me as a fish cop!
-D.N.R. *"fish cop"* **Officer 1995**

<u>*Trails*</u> – Deer, especially does and fawns, travel regular paths for long periods of time, often using the same routes between feeding and bedding areas.
Trails can become bare and trampled to the ground.

An old boy knows that if he finds and watches a well-worn trail littered with fresh tracks, sooner or latter he will see deer.

Upon scouting out a good trail or "run" you must be careful.

If deer pick up your scent on or around a run, they might quit using it and shift to another.

Therefore, don't walk along a deer run, and try not to cross one on you way to your stand.
Try to stay on the downwind side of the run.

Early in the morning and late in the evenings are the best times to watch for deer moving along runs, keeping in mind that at mid-day, most deer bed in cover.
Doe runs are easy to find. They are often trampled to the ground and wind throughout the timber.

Buck runs, however, are often faint and in dense, thick cover.

A buck likes to walk a straight-line path. During the rut you'll often find a buck sniffing around on the downwind side of a doe run.

The secret to using deer runs and learning the art of scouting them for stand placement, can and will play a large part in your success at bagging a wall hanger.

Scout for deer trails or "runs" with fresh tracks throughout the season. It takes constant monitoring to understand what the deer are up to. Jeff May, a hunting buddy of mine, uses a tree mounted night camera that snaps a picture based on heat and movement.
This little device has produced some amazing photos of deer activity on runs during the night.

This has helped Jeff in many ways. Besides getting a lot of cool pictures of deer, Jeff uses the camera for stand placement. Thus, Jeff has got a few nice wall hanging bucks in his den.

Buck Fever- Other names for this hunter nightmare are _Target panic, target freezing, and the big lock-up._
No matter what you call it in your neck of the woods, buck fever has happened to the best of us.

It can affect the experienced as well as the novice, and has caused many hunters to leave the sport for good.
Buck fever causes a shooter to freeze just before getting to where he wants to aim.

At this point the frustrated hunter either punches the trigger or simultaneously jerks the weapon.
I know of a hunter that got shaking so bad, he blacked out and fell from his stand.
Remember the safety belt I talked about earlier? It saved this hunters life!

I was in a conversation once while cleaning deer on buck fever. Amazingly, four out of the ten hunters stated that they only get buck fever while bow hunting.
When it came to gun hunting, they had no problems with getting off the shot.

All four stated that the fever commonly intensifies when the archer is under pressure.

A tough tournament shot or a shot at a big buck can trigger the "jerk and snatch" reaction.

The best cure for getting through buck fever is to stop shooting and learn how to aim again.

Go out to your practice target and set up about 10 yards away.
The first step is to draw your bow and aim at the target with your finger behind the trigger.

Try to relax as you let the sight pin float on the bulls eye for about 15 seconds, and then let down. Do this several times.
Once you've done this several times, you are ready for the next step.

Draw, aim, and rest your finger on the trigger and

aim again without shooting.
You wouldn't believe how many hunters will involuntarily shoot at this point.
If this happens, go back to step one.

Continue this "don't shoot" therapy until you feel like you can move to step three, which actually allows you to shoot while intently aiming.

As long as you continue to aim hard and squeeze, keep shooting. But if you punch or freeze up just one time, go back through the steps.
All in all, the best thing to cure buck fever is know your weapons and how to aim them.
Practice builds confidence, and confidence will lead to a good shot.
Don't panic, when you see your buck moving in on your target range, know that you have mastered the target aim.
When the big boy is in range, then you've done everything right.

Keep these thoughts in your head. "I have scouted, placed my stand, used odor control, and have outsmarted this buck. I will take aim, and I will bag this big boy. This deer is mine!" Shoot your deer and get ready for the bragging rights!

Odor Control – It is imperative that a hunter control and conceal his scent.

You can lay down human scent in a variety of ways.

Fox example, leather boots leak scent when you walk into a stand.

If you push a limb out of the way with your hand, you deposit your scent on it. Even trace scent like that can spook a seasoned buck.

For starters have good hygiene. Wash your hair and body with unscented soap.

Then wash your camouflage in an unscented detergent and store your clothes in plastic bags until you're ready to hunt.

Spray your hunting clothes with a scent killer.
Use a cover scent specific to your hunting area.
There are apple, solid earth, pine, just to name a
few.
And for heavens sake don't go tromping threw the
woods smelling like a bottle of old spice!

Chapter 9

How Smart Are Deer?
" Why do they call it the department of Interior when they are in charge of everything outdoors? "
-Travis Black 1998

So just how smart are deer? This has been the subject of many beer fests among deer hunters. Is an adult buck the craftiest quarry you'll find anywhere outdoors?

Or are deer in general really pretty stupid? All any

hunter can do is develop his own ideas.

My thoughts on this subject are that deer are not smart, but they can be fantastically clever. Whenever I get into a debate about how smart deer are, I always ask: "How come so many deer are killed on highways by cars?"

It is a well-known fact that about 500,000 deer are killed on highways each year.

So if deer were smart they'd know enough not to run into a car they see coming and have every chance to avoid.

A deer has to be pretty stupid to get knocked off by a tractor-trailer, especially in daylight.

That's just one example of plan stupidity. Now let's consider another that would seem to indicate an even greater lack of smarts. In northern states, during winters of heavy snow, whitetails herd into cedar swamps or other lowland thickets to escape the worst effects of blizzards and the extreme cold.

These are termed "yards" and they are used traditionally year after year.
The problem is that herds are confined to very small areas where available food is quickly consumed.

If the winters are hard and long many of the younger and weaker deer die of starvation.
The horror of all this is that in many instances there would be no starvation if the deer were smart enough to reason things out.

In many starvation areas deer die only a few hundred yards away from lowlands harboring plenty of browse that isn't utilized.

I have to ask myself, "Why weren't these deer smart enough to travel a very short distance and save themselves?"

However, being clever is something else. Let me state some examples of just how clever deer can be.

All wild game react dramatically when somebody starts hunting them.

In all the whitetail states most of the deer harvest is taken during the first few days of the gun season, then the kill rate drops drastically.

Deer that fed in fields close to farm homes all summer are gone shortly after the shots begin roaring during the season.

The buck that has survived in the proximity to man has learned there are times to avoid him, and those times come with the echo of gunfire.

For instance, deer are frequently almost tame in summer, exhibiting entirely different behavior patterns than in the fall.

Are deer getting smarter? Can it be that through recent generations of ever increasing gunning pressure deer have developed built in alarm systems that say, "be clever" in fall?

There is no question about it; deer hunting is different today than it was just a few years ago. The older bucks with the big racks didn't get that way by being stupid.

The stupid ones have all ended up in the freezers. These modern bucks are of a much more clever strain than the ones we hunted years ago.

This is one of the hardest things for today's deer hunter to accept.
It's a fact; today's bucks don't make the same mistakes made by the bucks of yesteryear.

It seems as though there can be only one explanation; today's deer are much more clever because of heredity.
Their basic trick today is to hide instead of running.

Basically, the main reason I wrote this chapter was not to pick on deer but to express one principle.

The reason the majority of hunters don't bag a buck seems to be fundamental.
Every hunt is a contest of wits with only two possible outcomes: either you get your deer or you don't.

Usually the hunter loses the game because he is a lot smarter but far less clever than his quarry.
The odds highly favor the deer because they know

every inch of relatively small area they live in year-round.

The hunter is in the same area only a few days each fall.
He normally doesn't score because he makes mistakes, does something wrong, and doesn't hunt hard enough.

Chapter 10

Where to Place Your Shot
"If bucks were dynamite, there wouldn't be enough here to blow your nose"
- **Alex Hartley 1982**

Knowing what represents the first good shot will make you a more aggressive and successful deer hunter.

Knowing when not to shoot will make you a more ethical deer hunter.
The maturity of a deer hunter can better be judged by the kinds of shoots he passes up than the size of bucks he has taken.

The following tips will help you evaluate every situation.

Sometimes decisions can be really tough, but knowing a good shot from a marginal one, and sticking to your choices, is a critical skill in doing the right thing.

We can all sit in our easy chairs and hold forth on exactly what we would have done differently if it had been us in the tree instead of another hunter, but, in reality, these decisions have to be made first, often under great personal pressure.

Making the right moves at the right times requires pre-planned actions.
If a hunter follows the following tips, he will not only improve his chances of a nice buck, but also improve his skills as an outdoorsman.

One of the shots most attempted is what is called the *screened by brush* shot. These shots can be ethical under two conditions.
First, the range was very short, ten yards or less for the bow hunter and well under 100 yards for the gun hunter, and the brush was close to the buck not close to the hunter.

When the brush is close to the deer even a slight deflection would still produce a good hit.
Second, you have to have some kind of an opening to work with.
The opening should be slightly larger for the bow hunter.

Never try to plow through the brush with an arrow.

A heavy bullet, however, is a different story. You can get away with a lot more brush busting with a heavy slug than with an easily deflected arrow, but again, the brush must be very close to the deer to reduce the amount of deflection that can occur and you should start with some type of an opening.

When a whitetail is walking straight toward you this is called the *straight on* shot. With this shot a gun hunter has several choices, however, none for the bow hunter.

From the frontal angle the brisket is well designed for deflecting any but the most perfectly placed arrow.

Gun hunters can either wait for a good broadside shot as the deer comes closer and offers a bigger target, or if the setting requires fast action he can place the sight right on the center of the deer's chest.

Either course of action will result in an ethical high percentage shot.

The best course of action for the bow hunter is to simply wait for the deer to offer a better shot.
In open timber settings, a buck walking straight towards you will likely turn off at some point within bow range, offering a good broadside-shot angle. Patience is a virtue when dealing with a straight-on buck.

A straight down spine shot as the deer passes under your stand is good if you can make it. This shot carries a high degree of risk for the bow hunter because the target is small and full penetration is often difficult to achieve if you miss the small target.

A miss will create a single lung hit, at best. Most bows impact high when shot almost straight down, so if you are determined to try this shot in the field make sure to practice it beforehand.

By aligning your bow with the spine of the deer when aiming, you can eliminate the effects of a high hit.

Gun hunters can ethically aim right for the spine in a location that will produce an entry to the deer's vitals.

The shock of the impact will bring the deer down, offering the opportunity for a very quick follow-up shot.
Even after a deer has gotten past your stand and is walking straightaway, there remain little ethical grounds for any type of shot.

What opportunity you have consists of a shot that enters to the side of the spine, back near the paunch and angles through the liver and then one lung.

It is a quick fatal shot, but you had better know the anatomy of a deer so you can instantly determine where to aim.

Trying to stop a walking deer by grunting or whistling is the best approach if the cover is open.
The only downside to this strategy is that you must be at full draw or have your finger on the guns trigger and ready to shoot as soon as the deer stops, or you'll have yourself a spooked deer.

In thick cover, where you're forced to wait until the deer steps into a narrow shooting lane, it may be difficult to stop it right where you need it.

All in all, the best shot for any weapon is the broadside shot.
A good heart or lung shot is sure to bring down the deer or allow a good blood trail to follow.

Chapter 11

How to Field Dress A Deer

"Ok, let me get this straight. I tell you all my secrets on how to kill a monster buck, and you write these tips in your book, get money, and I get a pound of your deer jerky and a six-pack of suds. Deal!"
- **Flathead 2000**

It's a dirty job but someone has to do it! The timely removal of your deer's innards is often necessary to ensure untainted meat, and it also helps by reducing the weight you'll have to drag back to your truck or camp.

I have broken this procedure down to the following 13 steps:

1. If you're in an area that uses tags, tag your deer immediately. The tag must remain with the deer at all times, or you risk dealing with the *Fish cops.*
2. Carefully cut a circle around the anus so it's free and can be removed from within. Some hunters tie it off with string to prevent its contents from tainting the meat.

3. Remove and discard the testicles and cut the penis free so that it can be removed by the same route as the anus.
4. Beginning close to the pelvis, open the stomach cavity to the ribcage. After starting the cut, use the first two fingers of your other hand to help guide the knife, you must only cut through skin and a thin layer of meat, avoiding the entrails.

5. Cut through the ribs and skin, following the breastbone, on up to the neck. This is no problem with a sharp knife, but don't twist the blade while it's between the bones; a brittle knife blade could easily break if twisted.

6. Continue cutting on up to the base of the skull.

7. Sever the windpipe and esophagus at the base of the skull.

8. Cut the diaphragm loose. This is the sheet of muscle that separates the stomach area from the chest cavity.

9. Allow the deer to roll on its side, and "help" the organs to come out. You'll have to pull a little, but they should be mostly free.

10.   Be extremely careful in removing the bladder! You must reach up into the pelvis and pinch it shut while you cut it free with the other hand. If any urine is spilled on the meat, remove it immediately with water or snow, or a clean cloth.

11.   Clean any debris from the cavity. Any stomach contents or other substances should be removed as quickly as possible.
12.   Separate the heart and liver if you, or someone you know, likes to eat them. Cloth bags are recommended for keeping these clean and allowing them to cool.
13.   Start dragging your deer out. If you do not have a quad runner, or a deer cart. I recommend a plastic sheet sled; they make a big difference on the old back!

If you plan to have your deer mounted, don't cut above the ribcage.
You'll have to reach up through the ribcage to cut the esophagus and windpipe.
Leave the caping (the skinning of the head & neck) to a taxidermist.

When opening the stomach cavity, slip two fingers of your opposite hand underneath the sheet of muscle you're cutting through, and pull it away from the entrails.

Try to use only an inch or so of your knife blade. If you will be skinning and quartering your deer within a couple of hours of the kill, you might be ahead not to field dress it.

That way, you won't have sticks, leaves, and other debris to clean off.

It also helps to keep flies off on warm fall days.

When field dressing a deer, I recommend the use of latex gloves. You can buy them at any medical supply store and they help with infections you might get if you should have a few cuts or scrapes on your hands.

Chapter 12

Tips, Tips, and More Tips
"Rick, teach me how to kill a big deer with horns."
-Tim Brown 2001

This chapter is nothing but tricks of the trade. It is full of tips from hunters that have learned the art of deer hunting through time and experience. Like I stated in the beginning of this book, if you learn one thing that helps to bag the monster buck of your dreams, then this book was worth every cent you paid.

- If you are looking for a hunting outfitter and guide, try attending a few gun shows and outdoor expo's. You can usually find outfitters and guides booths at these shows.

By talking face to face with your prospective outfitter or guide you will be able to get a better feel for them and a lot more information than you would get from an ad, or over the phone.

- For packing out your deer, a 4 wheeler is great for getting your deer out of the timber. The best type is with a winch.

- Some hunters keep a 4x4 plastic tarp folded up in their daypacks. After dressing out the deer, they wrap the deer in the tarp and drag him out. The tarp keeps the dirt and debris out and the deer slides along the ground a lot smoother.

- Another way to get your big buck out of the timber is by using a plastic sled. After you field dress the deer use the sled to drag him out of the timber. The sled is much easier to pull and it also helps keep dirt and debris off. They are very inexpensive, light to carry and they are sold almost everywhere.

- Keep rain, snow, mud and dirt out of your barrel by putting a piece of tape over the end of it. The tape will blow off because of the escaping gasses before the bullet gets to it. The tape will not affect your accuracy.

- Air currents carrying your scent can have a big effect on your deer hunting. Try carrying a small squeeze bottle filled with unscented talcum powder. If you can't figure out which way the wind is blowing just hold it up and give a little squeeze. The drift of the powder will instantly give you the wind direction.

- Tape one end of sewing thread, about 12 inches long, to the end of your barrel or

bow. Frequently check the thread to see which way the wind is blowing. Always hunt into the wind.

- The next time you are in the timber scouting, pick up fallen acorns from the ground. Put the acorns in water and boil them until they are soft. Smash up the acorns and then boil them again. When the water turns real dark in color, strain the mixture and put the liquid away until your next hunt. Put the mixture in a spray bottle for easy application. You now have an effective and all natural cover scent.

- If you use a scent drag rag when approaching your deer stand, try circling your stand about 20 yards away. From the front of your stand place a scent saturated cotton ball at the 10 and 2 o'clock positions. This will allow the deer that do follow your scent trail some place to stop and pause, allowing a good broadside shot while bow hunting. Naturally this tactic can be used while gun hunting, just allow a little more distance from your stand to your scent balls and scent trail.

- Before going into the timber take an empty film canister and fill it half full with cotton balls. Then poke two holes in the lid big enough so the scent can get out. Next, put a string through one of the holes and tie a knot so the lid is held to the string. Then put your favorite scent in the film canister and put the lid back on. When you get to the timber tie the string to a limb about 7 feet up. Use several film canisters for different scents.

- When hunting deer, deer hunters often use scent free clothing. But how many hunters keep their guns scent free? If you are good to your gun chances are that you clean your barrel with solvents and use a lot of oil to keep your gun in good shape. That could be some of the most potent scent a hunter carries with him on a hunt. Try using a gunbrella (a cloth gun protector that wraps around your gun and scope) sprayed with your favorite cover scent. This will eliminate a lot of the scent and you're bound to see more bucks.

- For a cheap and easy cover scent buy some all-natural popcorn with no additives like butter, cheese, or caramel. Salt is all right. All you do is pop the corn and roll the bag up and take it with you. Make sure popcorn is not burnt. You may think it will be bulky but you can crush the popcorn. When you get to your stand, open the bag and fluff it

back up. When the hunt is over, just dump the popcorn out for the deer to eat and make sure you bring back your bag to keep the timber clean.

- After washing your hunting clothes in scent free detergent, put them in a plastic garbage bag. Then buy some natural potting soil. Empty the potting soil into the garbage bag with your hunting clothes and let it sit for a week or so before hunting season. When you get ready to go home, put your hunting clothes back into the garbage bag with the potting soil and they will be ready to go when you go out next.

- One major mistake hunters do every season is spend a week getting their hunting clothes smelling like soil and leaves, and then smoke in their trucks or eat at a greasy spoon for breakfast, wearing the clothes they tried to cover the scent with. Do not smoke or eat in a café while wearing the clothes you plan on hunting in the timber with. If you do, you just wasted your time and efforts.

- To keep unwanted scent off your hunting boots never wear them for anything other than hunting or scouting. Never wear your hunting boots to work or even to fill up with gas before or after your hunt. Rubber boots work the best; they won't pick up foreign scent like leather does.

- If you're a smoker and a hunter, you know that you cannot smoke in your blind or

stand. Try using the patch along with the gum, this will knock out your craving for nicotine and keep you in your stand calmer and longer.

- Nothing is worse than the cold air of walking during hunting season, causing your nose to plug up. One thing I highly recommend is the use of **BREATHERIGHT** strips. They keep your air passage clear allowing your nose not to plug up.

- Place peanut butter on a tree branch and deer will come up and lick it off the tree.

- When tracking deer on snow, always be aware that deer often tend to circle back to see what is following them.

- Big bucks tend to make their scrapes on high ground.

- No matter how good your spot is, don't hunt there on consecutive days. You stand an excellent chance of contaminating the area with your scent.

- The route a deer takes can often tell you what the sex is. Large bucks tend to go over and around large obstructions. Does are likely to crawl under a fallen tree or weave through a thicket.

- Do not spend a lot of time hunting rubs and scrapes during the rut because bucks move in a totally unpredictable patterns during this time.

- Most big bucks are shot on the downwind side of a food source.

- If you would like to excite a buck in your hunting area, consider taking soil from a

  scrape in another area and placing it in a scrape near your stand. Be careful not to leave any human scent.

- One study concludes that over 95% of the scrapes bucks made in an area would be used again the next year.

- Since most heat escapes through the head, a little baking soda in the hat would help eliminate any odors escaping with the heat and moisture.

- Did you know that in the early days of the American Frontier the skin of a male deer was worth a dollar? This is we got the term "buck" for a $1 bill.

- A great tool for blood trailing is a fluorescent painted clothespin. As you follow the blood trail, simply clip these highly visible clothespins onto branches or bushes. They are a quick and easy way to keep track of the "line of flight" of the deer.

- If hunting along a fence-row, tie a fence area down. Since deer take paths of the least resistance, bucks will jump over the tied down part. This will enable you to ambush him at the location you want.

- Practice you're climbing and shooting with all your equipment on. This allows for any uncomfortable conditions to be dealt with before the onslaught of the hunting season.

- When hunting a new area it pays, in the long run, to hunt a new stand each day for a while. This is the fastest way to learn the deer movement patterns.

- If you are going to bow hunt from a tree stand, practice shooting from a tree stand.

  One major mistake hunter's do is practice tree stand shooting from the ground. It's not the same.

- After shooting a deer. Wait for it to die. Many hunters make the big mistake of chasing down a freshly shot deer that has not hit the ground. A wounded buck can run for miles.

- Do not leave your stand until the legal shooting time is over. Probably the best time of the day to kill a buck is the last minute of shooting light.

- If you are going to hunt a large field or food plot, hunt it in the evening.

- If you don't have any faith in a deer call, afraid of scaring deer away, only use it after you see a deer that you are not going to shoot. You will get to see that it doesn't scare them, and you will get to see their reactions. Make sure to use the appropriate call, or you might confirm to yourself that they don't work

- On the first day of deer season, a good idea is to sneak into the timber early. Then just sit tight until daylight. The most hunters in the woods are on the first two days of hunting, thus the deer start running early.

- When hunting on public grounds, the smart hunter will pattern the other hunters' movements. Be in the sanctuaries the deer will seek when disturbed by the mass amount of hunters in the timber.

- Another inexpensive masking scent is baking soda. Always wash your hunting clothes in baking soda to kill odor. Also take a small spray bottle; add baking soda and warm water. Shake it well and take it with you. Spray yourself every hour or so.

Chapter 13

My Favorite Venison Recipes
" As I promised. Here a few venison recipes from my venison cook book!"
-Rick

Now that your ready to ***"BAG'EM & TAG'EM,"*** You're going to need to know how to cook your deer.

As I stated at the beginning of this book, here are a few recipes from my venison cookbook.

Cooking deer should be as much fun as hunting them.

I will give a few tips and recipes from each chapter to help you get started.

Travis's Slow Cooker Venison Stew

- 3 lbs. Venison
- 6 medium potatoes
- 5 carrots
- 3 stalks celery
- 1 large onion
- 2 cloves garlic
- 10 brown bouillon cubes

Cut venison into 1-inch chunks. Roll in flour until coated all around. Cube potatoes, carrots, celery, onions and garlic.

Brown venison in oil until half brown. Add 10 bouillon cubes and 3 cups of hot water to skillet and simmer for 2 minutes.

Scrape meat and gravy from skillet and add to slow cooker. Add all vegetables and stir together with meat and add 3 more cups of hot water.

Cook on high for six hours. Add cornstarch to thicken as needed.

Deer Camp Chili

- 5 table spoons of bacon drippings
- 3 lbs of ground venison
- 2 large chopped onions
- 3 minced garlic cloves
- 2 chopped bell peppers
- 3 chopped jalapeno peppers

- 2 can tomatoes
- 16 oz tomato sauce
- 1 tablespoon ground cumin
- 1 tablespoon paprika
- 1 cup water
- 32 oz chili beans
- 1 shot whiskey

Heat bacon drippings in a large heavy pot. Add meat and cook until slightly browned.
Add onions, garlic, bell peppers, jalapeno peppers, and sauté until limp.

Add tomatoes, tomato sauce, chili powder, cumin, paprika, whiskey, salt and pepper. Stir to blend.

Add water and simmer about 30 minutes. Add beans and continue to cook about 45 more minutes.

Venison and Barley soup

- 2 deer shanks
- 1 cup barley, pearl
- 1 cup peas, green split
- 2 onions, chopped
- 2 garlic clove, finely chopped
- 1 bell pepper, seeded, chopped
- 14 cups beef stock
- 5 tablespoons butter
- 2 tablespoons salt
- 1 tablespoon pepper
- 1 bay leaf

Brown garlic, onion and pepper in butter. Add venison, cut into 1-inch pieces and brown lightly.

Add stock and remaining ingredients and bring to a boil.

Cover and simmer for 2-3 hours, until meat is tender.
Season according to taste.

John's Venison Hash

- 5 tablespoons bacon drippings
- 1 large yellow onion, chopped
- 5 lbs chopped venison roast
- 8 medium potatoes, diced
- 4 tablespoons flour

- 2 cloves minced garlic
- 5 cups beef broth
- 1 tablespoon pepper
- 1 tablespoon seasoned salt
- ½ tablespoon chili powder

Brown onion and potatoes in the bacon fat.
Add flour and brown.

Add broth and other ingredients.
Let simmer until tender.

Hunters Choice Venison Tenderloin Steaks

- 6 loin steaks ¼ inch thick
- ½ cup seasoned flour
- Salt and pepper
- Olive oil

Roll each steak in flour until coated. Add salt and pepper.

Cover the bottom of a large fry pan with olive oil.
Fry steaks on medium heat until nicely brown, turn and fry until juices are clear.

Turn steaks again from time to time to make sure they are tender and mild.

Dad's Mustard Fried Venison Steak

- 6 loin steaks ¾ inch thick
- ¼ teaspoon garlic powder
- ¼ teaspoon season salt
- ¼ teaspoon pepper
- 4 tablespoons Dijon mustard
- 2 teaspoons horseradish
- 1 ½ cup olive oil

Season steaks with the dry seasonings.

Combine mustard and horseradish.

Spread mixture on each side of the steaks so that the steaks are fully covered on both sides.

Fry in hot olive oil.
Poke with fork and as soon as juices run clear, steaks are done.

Serve with green salad and baked potato.

Venison Steak and Gravy

- 3 lbs venison cube steak
- 1 large yellow onion
- 3 packages of brown gravy mix

In a large skillet, brown the cube steak.
After browning, arrange the steaks in a 13x9x2
inch-baking pan.

Chop the onion and add in to the steak gravy
according to the package directions.

Pour the gravy over the onion.

Cover with foil and bake at 400 degrees for 1
hour.

Serve with hash browns.

Venison Tenderloin of the Peppercorn

- 4 cloves of minced garlic
- 1 venison loin
- 3 tablespoons coarsely crushed whole peppercorns
- 2 tablespoons butter
- 1 tablespoon of seasoning salt

Spread garlic over the venison loin and then roll the loin in the peppercorn.

Put the loin in a preheated oven at 425 degrees and bake for 15 minutes.

Then dot the loin with butter and continue baking for 20 more minutes.

Let the tenderloin stand for 5 minutes before slicing.

My First Jerky

- 5 lbs 1/8 inch sliced venison
- 4 tablespoons hickory smoked salt
- 2 tablespoons garlic salt
- 2 tablespoons Monosodium glutamate
- 4 tablespoons seasoned pepper
- 1 cup soy sauce
- ½ cup Worcester sauce
- 1 teaspoon accent

Mix all dry ingredients together while oven is warming to 200 degrees.

Sprinkle meat with the dry mixture on both sides. Drape meat on oven racks.

Place the oven racks in oven with door open 2 inches.

After one hour, baste with mixed sauces, repeating every ½ hour for about two hours.

Then drop oven heat to 170 degrees and finish meat in about 1-½ hours.

Grand Pappy's Deer Jerky

- 7 lbs of venison roast
- 1 tablespoon salt
- ¼ tablespoon black pepper
- ¼ teaspoon white pepper
- 1 teaspoon red pepper
- 1 tablespoon meat tenderizer
- 2 tablespoons seasoned salt
- 2 teaspoons accent
- 1 teaspoon garlic powder
- 1tablespoon kitchen bouquet
- 2 tablespoons Morton tender quick
- ½ cup Worcestershire sauce
- 1/3 cup soy sauce
- 1/3 cup barbecue sauce
- 1/3 cup liquid smoke

Cut meat in thin slices. Combine salt, peppers, meat tenderizers, seasoned salt, accent, garlic and onion powders, kitchen bouquet, Morton tender quick, Worcestershire sauce, soy sauce, barbecue sauce and liquid smoke.

Marinate meat in sauce for 24 hours in a seal able plastic bag. Place meat directly on oven racks, line bottom of oven with foil, or rack in a shallow pan and dry in oven for 6-8 hours on low setting.

Right-A-Way-Ranch jerky Meat

- 4 lbs of lean venison roast or loins
- 1 can cola (not diet)
- 10 ounces Worcestershire sauce
- 10 ounces teriyaki sauce
- 3 tablespoons liquid smoke
- 4 tablespoons black ground pepper
- 3 tablespoons brown sugar
- 1 tablespoon garlic powder

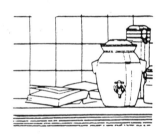

Cut meat into ¼ inch thick slices. Combine all ingredients. Place meat and ingredients into a plastic zip lock bags and marinate meat overnight.

Place meat in a smoker and smoke according to smoker instructions.

Or use the dehydrator or oven methods.

The Duke's Pickled Venison Heart

- 1 deer heart
- ½ teaspoon brown sugar
- 3 small white onions
- ½ quart cold water
- ½ teaspoon black pepper
- ½ teaspoon salt
- ½ tablespoon garlic salt
- Apple vinegar

Set aside 1-quart jar. Boil deer heart in a large pan filled with enough water to cover the heart.

When the water starts to boil add brown sugar and boil until cooked.
Drain heart and cool in the refrigerator.

Mix onions and meat and place in quart jar. Add ½ quart of cold water.
Put in salt, garlic powder and pepper. Finish filling jar with apple vinegar.

Place cover on jar, shake and place in the refrigerator for 3 days.

12 Pointer Deer Loaf

- 2 ½ lbs deer burger
- 1 large yellow onion
- 1 bell pepper
- 2 eggs
- 1 cup bread crumbs
- 1 garlic clove
- 3 tablespoons chili powder
- Seasonings, salt and pepper
- 1 can tomato sauce
- 4 strips of bacon

Mix the first 8 ingredients and put in a greased baking dish.

Place bacon strips on top of loaf. Pour the tomato sauce over all.

Bake at 350 degrees for 1 ½ hours or until done.

To Order Copies

Please send me _____ copies of
BAG EM' and **TAG EM'**: $9.95 each
plus $2.00 S/H. (Make checks payable
to Black Iron Cookin'.)

Name _____

Street _____

City _____ State _____ Zip _____

Black Iron Cookin' Co.
1854 - 345th Avenue
Wever IA   52658
1-800-571-2665

- -

To Order Copies

Please send me _____ copies of
BAG EM' and **TAG EM'**: $9.95 each
plus $2.00 S/H. (Make checks payable
to Black Iron Cookin'.)

Name _____

Street _____

City _____ State _____ Zip _____

Black Iron Cookin' Co.
1854 - 345th Avenue
Wever IA   52658
1-800-571-2665